M000284199

TEN TINY TRUTHS

PRINCIPLES FOR LIVING A BIG LIFE

because
with the truth
you can make
a difference

TEN TINY TRUTHS

PRINCIPLES FOR LIVING A BIG LIFE

Copyright © 2020 Erin Anderson, Live Big Co.

All rights reserved. No part of this publication may be reproduced, distributed, or transmitted in any form or by any means, including photocopying, recording, digital scanning, or other electronic or mechanical methods, without the prior written permission of the publisher, except in the case of brief quotations embodied in critical reviews and certain other uses permitted by copy-write law. For permission requests, please contact hello@livebigco.com.

Cover design by Erin Anderson
Cover artwork by Sarah Gold
Book design by Erin Anderson
Photography by Jessie McNaught, Andi Wardrop & Darby Magill

Contact the author: www.livebigco.com

Hardcover ISBN: 978-1-7774592-0-8

First printing 2020

FOR MY MUM GAIL
A true original.

PRINCIPLES

ONE   **YOU HAVE A SONG TO SING**

TWO   **90% OF LIFE IS SHOWING UP**

THREE   **RISE TO THE OCCASION**

FOUR   **DON'T TRY HARD, GET REAL**

FIVE   **BE A FOUNTAIN NOT A DRAIN**

SIX   **PERFECT IS BORING**

SEVEN   **CONTRIBUTION HAPPENS IN THE NOW**

EIGHT   **YOU ARE ALWAYS INFLUENCING**

NINE   **FORGIVE TO LIVE BIG**

TEN   **TINY JOYS CREATE A BIG LIFE**

A birdsong can
even, for a moment,
make the whole world
into a sky within us,
because we feel that the bird
does not distinguish between
its heart and the world's.

- RAINER MARIA RILKE

IN THE BEGINNING

Every morning my mum would send me off to school chiming "Now, get out there and make a difference!" Her relentless message was met with my classic teenage eye roll.

Despite my self-absorbed teenage years followed by a decade of wallowing in my twenties, I eventually became inspired to let her message in. It took failure, suffering, loneliness, and despair to see the wisdom in her teachings. I thought that getting out there and making a difference would require two things that I didn't have: an overflowing cup to give from and having my whole life together.

What I began to realize is simply this: making a difference is when love meets action.

When I paused long enough, I realized I was a witness to that dynamic combination of love and action all my life. My father was an athlete and an advocate for fitness and healthy living. He created the Jackrabbit Cross Country Ski Program for kids in Winnipeg Manitoba where I grew up. On weekends, he'd host Lycra wearing, rough and rugged athletes in our home, encouraging and empowering them to go the extra mile. He did the same on the lake, in the mountains, and on the ski hill. My dad, known in my family as "Uncle Sport" showed what patient and loving leadership looked like. He loved competition but was never out to win. His focus was always on what he could give, inspire, and create. Being inducted into the Manitoba Sports Hall of Fame was a platform for him, not a trophy.

My mother Gail was an ultra connector. She made a difference with every person she met. If you met her, she would find out what makes you unique and wonderful within the first ten minutes. Then she'd think of three other people who you'd resonate with and introduce you to them. Quite often, she'd find you so compelling and interesting that she'd befriend you and make you dinner. If you commented on one of her paintings, she'd likely pull it off the wall in that very moment and give it to you. She'd insist.

Both my parents valued people for who they really are. They saw the best in people and treated everyone with respect and kindness. They embodied "get out there and make a difference" without requiring recognition or praise for doing it, which is why I think I missed their message for most of my life. I thought that making a difference would require me to be great, special, and remarkable. It sure seemed like my parents had all three of those things in them. Now I realize they were simply being themselves, following their passions and dreams, and making a difference along the way. Today the message I ignored for so long seems so simple and so true.

Yet the thing about these kinds of truthful messages, is they are sometimes invisible. And when they become known, they need to be repeated, lived, broken, forgotten, abandoned, and trampled on before landing in our hearts and minds in a way that makes sense.

School was a social structure for me, a container to discover who I was in this micro society. Classrooms were endured, often feared, and were not the place where I thrived. Learning by memorization or explanation didn't work for me.

I tried to try. I had an earnest desire to be like the other kids who studied and got A's. I slowly discovered that for me learning came through experience. I had to feel it in my bones to really get it, and then I never forgot it. Embodied learning just made sense. I not only got it but I could also turn around and teach it.

The perfect, simple story to describe the embodied learning experience goes like this:

One day you walk down the street and fall into a hole.

Dusting yourself off, you climb out. Assessing your bruises, you carry on.

The next day you walk down the street, see the hole, but you fall in it anyway.

Baffled, you once again dust yourself off and carry on.

The third day you walk down the street, you see the hole, pause, and walk around it. You're feeling pretty good about yourself now.

The fourth day you take a different street.

The point of the story is that deep, spiritual learning, the kind that lands in your bones and being, may produce some bruises. It's not preferential nor is it usually comfortable.

Eyes open, willing to fall, we carry on. Because the truth is, if we're not learning, we're not growing.

It took me years to understand that "get out there and make a difference" was the foundation of a truthful life because I learned it through experience. I had to embody it. Yet even in its simplicity, I still wonder why it took so long for me to understand it?

I believe we like to dramatize, conceptualize, and complicate matters then point blame when things don't work out. I've certainly done that. My mum never did. She was the most personally responsible person I ever knew, despite being dealt a difficult hand.

From the time she was six months old, her mum was confined to a wheelchair. She never knew what it was like to be rocked to sleep, picked up and carried, or held in the loving arms of her mother. At five years old, she was sent to boarding school where she slept alone in her dorm room. There were no long cuddles or bedtime stories. To this day, I marvel that she became such an attentive, creative, and nurturing mom to us. Growing up, we had arts and crafts stations, homemade lunches every day, and full on winter wonderland Christmases.

Throughout my mum's life she developed cancer four times, overcoming all but the last bout. Right up until the moment she left her body, my mum remained optimistic, loving, and pragmatic.

Her pragmatism extended to her directive of how she wanted to be remembered. She had an aversion to grand gestures or conceptual descriptive language. She made us promise not to honour her as "a remarkable woman who transcended through the portal."

She was a lover of what's true and important. She wasn't concerned about being remembered, she was focused on us, her kids and husband. She was masterful at putting her love and attention on what was real—what was in front of her in the moment.

Many of the principles in this book came from her, my original teacher. She would be so happy to know all her lessons sank in and that I am passing them on to you.

These principles are now in my bones. They provide guidance in times of confusion or doubt. Each one has been taught, learned, and discovered throughout my life. I never look at them as rules or something to get right; I see them as river banks that help me flow in the right direction. What I know for sure is that these principles have prevented me from falling into a hole many, many times.

The definition of a principle is a fundamental truth or proposition that serves as the foundation for a system of beliefs or behaviours or a chain of reasoning.

My hope is that these ten principles will provide you with an opportunity to shift your perspective, access a new belief, and upgrade your life. You have a big life to live and people to contribute to, and I am certain that this book's purpose is to support you along your journey.

You can use this book as a coach in your corner, ready to give you what you need in the moment.

This tiny book was written for you and in honour of my mother. It is my deepest hope and intention that you'll use it when you forget who you are, that you'll reach for it when you're in a pickle and need something solid to rely on. With this book, I hope you feel like you're in good company.

These principles have provided spiritual and practical guidance for me as I've navigated the many ups and downs of my life.

You have a big life one constructed from the love you show, the relationships you build, and the contribution you are to others. Now, get out there and make a difference.

Instructions for living a life.
Pay attention. Be astonished.
Tell about it.

- MARY OLIVER

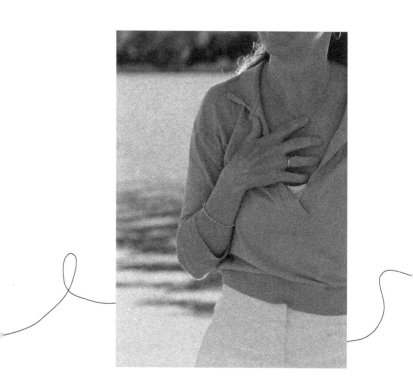

ONE

YOU HAVE A
SONG TO SING

YOU HAVE A SONG TO SING

Author, speaker, and leader Dr. Wayne Dyer once said, *"Don't die with your music still inside you."* Hearing this rocked me to my core. The idea of living with a message, a service, a contribution unexpressed felt heavy and full of regret.

Regret feels like a bear trap around my heart.

The path to regret is paved with doubt. Should I? Shouldn't I? Who am I to do it? What if...? These are the nuts and bolts of regret.

The quote from the Gospel of St. Thomas pinched my soul awake: *"If you bring forth what is within you, what you bring forth will save you. If you do not bring forth what is within you, what you do not bring forth will destroy you."*

The truth is, there is a thin veil between you and your song, and it's the veil of doubt and drama.

The last time you belted out a show tune in the shower, did you feel held back by concerns of comparison and failure? Probably not.

Of course, the world is a different stage compared to the privacy of your shower. Yet when you own that you are the same person in public as you are in private, you may be more inclined to sing out loud no matter where you are.

A client I was working with was immersed in discovering her voice and her message while leading a group of people through a training. We spoke right before she went into her last session. It was primed to be a powerful moment of completion and celebration. Instead of feeling excited, she found herself in the grips of doubt and concern.

She had forgotten her song.

She identified that she needed to be reminded of who she was at the core of her being. I asked her to place her hand on her heart and say out loud "I AM LIGHT AND LOVE."

On the other end of the phone, I could hear her shuffling. She said, "Just a moment, I'm standing by a coffee shop window, I need to move before people see me do this."

It struck me. Why are we so concerned about people seeing us be magnificent? Why was she worried about people seeing her place her hand on her heart, declaring who she really was?

Your song will inspire people to rise up and sing their own song.

My hope is that we create a world where more people walk through the streets with their hand on their heart, greeting people with who they really are.

This lovely parable helps illustrate how we seem to miss our unique gifts:

An elderly Chinese woman had two large pots, each hung on the ends of a pole which she carried across her neck. One of the pots had a crack in it while the other pot was perfect and always delivered a full portion of water.

At the end of the long walks from the stream to the house, the cracked pot arrived only half full. For a full two years this went on daily, with the woman bringing home only one and a half pots of water. Of course, the perfect pot was proud of its accomplishments. But the poor cracked pot was ashamed of its own imperfection, and miserable that it could only do half of what it had been made to do. After two years of what it perceived to be bitter failure, it spoke to the woman one day by the stream.

"I am ashamed of myself, because this crack in my side causes water to leak out all the way back to your house."

The old woman smiled, "Did you notice that there are flowers on your side of the path, but not on the other pot's side? That's because I have always known about your flaw, so I planted flower seeds on your side of the path, and every day while we walk back, you water them. For two years I have been able to pick these beautiful flowers to decorate the table. Without you being just the way you are, there would not be this beauty to grace the house."

There is such a striving for smooth, glossy perfection that people don't let their hearts break or their pots leak. There is an editing, manicuring, posturing that's taken hold of people's spirits to the point that they live in fear of themselves. We are told endless contradictions that block the channel to our spirit's message. We are told to stay in our lane but be an innovator, follow the formula but stand out, do like I do but don't copy me.

And meanwhile, your pot is cracked anyway, you just have to see the beauty that is created because of it.

In all the confusion, there is an epidemic of inauthenticity. People find themselves zig zagging to please others or to seem like a good person. They go to bed at night not really knowing or loving themselves.

Singing your own song is the very nature of being true to yourself. This unique gift that each of us has is our own and nobody else's. When you know the song you're here to sing, you'll also know the song you are NOT here to sing.

All that there is to do is claim it and sing from the rooftops!

What is growing because of the leak in your pot?

What are you most proud of yourself for?

What do your biggest fans say about you?

What makes you jump for joy?

What moves you to tears in a wonderful way?

If you had a signature song, what would its title be?

TWO

90% OF LIFE
IS SHOWING UP

90% OF LIFE IS SHOWING UP

I was raised by this principle and I believe it's the one that ignites all the other principles in life.

There have been many occasions when I've chosen not to show up. The narrative in my head is defensive and full of predictions, assumptions, and complaints about the occasion. "I'm quite certain that I'm not needed," "it will be dull," "I don't have the energy," "it's not worth the time or effort."

There have been dinner parties, costume parties, and fundraising galas that I haven't shown up to.

The narrative between prediction and doubt is not cute.

Showing up is a decision made before the laundry list of what you'd rather be doing begins to run in your head. Showing up requires faith and commitment. Showing up is physical and tangible. Showing up may come easily and it may require all you've got, it's an unconditional principle.

Showing up is not a concept or idea, it's an act of integrity.

The truth is, if you're not showing up in life, you're hiding from it. And when you hide from life, you'll miss the magic of it.

When I question the purpose of showing up, it gives me the illusion that I have control over my life. This is the myth my ego wants me to believe. The ego—the part of us that wants to keep us home on the couch where it's safe— doesn't always have our best interests at heart. It's when we relinquish our need for comfort and decide to show up to life, that is when we grow.

On the other side of control is possibility.

Showing up is not about saying Yes to everything and faking it. Fully showing up in life requires a hefty dose of self-awareness. It also requires knowing what you are a Yes for. Knowing what you're a Yes for is understanding what truly lights you up versus what drains you. On the other side of your Yes is a No. For example, saying Yes to show up for a gathering means you're also saying No to a quiet evening with family.

Creating awareness around what calls you to action allows you to show up authentically and fully while honoring your No.

Woody Allen once said that "80% of success in life is just showing up." My mum simplified it and took it up a notch. 90% of life is showing up.

THE PRACTICE

By not showing up, what am I missing out on?

What limiting thoughts have I placed on what has yet to happen?

What will the cost be if I don't show up?

What can I contribute to others by showing up?

CREATE A LIST OF WHAT YOU SHOW UP FOR

I show up for my friends
I show up for my family
I show up for life celebrations

I show up for _____

I show up for _____

I show up for _____

I show up for _____

My mission in life is not merely to survive,
but to thrive; and to do so with some
passion, some compassion, some
humour, and some style.

- MAYA ANGELOU

THREE

RISE TO THE OCCASION

RISE TO THE OCCASION

I first heard the phrase *rise to the occasion* from my mum. It was something she reminded me to do all my life. It lifted me, pushed me forward, and encouraged me to show up wholeheartedly, as I am, for all of life's occasions.

Open your eyes wide and you'll see that occasions are everywhere. They are a part of your daily routine - walking your dog, making breakfast for your kids, leading a team, teaching a yoga class, or simply getting out of bed in the morning. You have the delightful responsibility of elevating each moment. If you rise, it will sound like this: "I get to walk my dog today" or "I get to make breakfast for my kids today." Once you show up, and do so in an upgraded way, that's where the magic happens. If you wait for others to dazzle you or meet your expectations or meet the right conditions, you'll miss the occasion.

Rising to the occasion is an act that calls on your courage. These are the moments you consciously step out of your comfort zone where there is no clear picture of what will occur.

The unknown cannot be met with expectations or limitations. You cannot rise perfectly or according to a plan. The work is in making a choice, saying yes, and showing up.

But what about the occasions that suck? There is no doubt that each and every one of us has been knocked down a time or two. Each blow was unexpected and unwanted, and likely undeserved. I imagine if you're tracing your memory back to those dark days you'll recall the journey was bumpy. You may not have been proud of your actions or you may be harbouring some anger and resentment about it.

You may also reflect that the moment the pain eased up and you got to the other side of it you were stronger and wiser.

The night my mother died she stayed true to her message. I had been with my mum in her final days, a gift I will never take for granted. It was the emotional equivalent to climbing Mount Everest, no turning back and deep crevasses everywhere. During a conversation on that final night I let her know I had to lead a workshop the next morning and I wasn't sure how I was going to be able to pull it off. She said, in her pragmatic and direct way, "Oh Erie, rise to the occasion!"

I showed up to that workshop with football eyes, saw each participant, looked at my notes, took a deep breath, and began to rise to the occasion.

This principle is here to ask you to get up on your tippy toes and reach up, elevating this very moment. It's encouraging you to step out into the unknown and into possibility.

There are occasions to rise to everyday. The sluggish mind of the ego will provide a very compelling argument about why you shouldn't. The narrative is an easy one to keep alive and on repeat.

Our minds are governed by two rulers: The Ego and The Spirit. The Ego wants us to be safe and small, it begs "No risks please." Our Spirit wants us to soar.

The Ego's function from the moment we became human has been to protect us. The dictionary's definition of ego is *the part of the mind that mediates between the conscious and the unconscious and is responsible for reality testing and a sense of personal identity.* Responsible for reality testing and sense of personal identity! Now that's a big job.

In a world of unknowns, our ego can only test reality based on the past.

Does this narrative sound familiar?

You: *Should I go to the event?*

Ego: *Let me check the files. Nope, don't go, you went to an event once and you saw your ex boyfriend and it was embarrassing. Don't go. Not safe.*

This happens quickly, so fast in fact that you have no idea where your thoughts came from. But something inside of you knows these are not the thoughts and feelings that will lead to your big life.

Your big life is waiting for you on the other side of resistance, it's time to rise up.

ERIN ANDERSON

THE PRACTICE

ASK NEW QUESTIONS THAT WILL INVOKE YOUR SPIRIT TO ANSWER AND HAVE YOUR EGO TAKE THE BACK SEAT:

What would make me feel alive?

What is a new action I can take right now?

If wonder and amazement live in the unknown, what's an unknown I can step into now?

Instead of sinking back into the couch, what occasion can I rise to now?

When I slow down and get very quiet, what do I know I want?

Don't ask yourself what the world needs.
Ask what makes you come alive and go
do it. Because what the world needs
is more people who have come alive.

- HOWARD THURMAN

FOUR

DON'T TRY HARD, GET REAL

DON'T TRY HARD, GET REAL

I met my future father-in-law the year before he died.
While he was battling lung cancer, my boyfriend (now-
husband) and I went to visit. We were excited to share how
our relationship had grown and how we were about to buy
a house and move in together.

Sean was my dream man, someone who I hoped and
prayed would come into my life. He fit the picture I held
since the days my University best friend and I would flip
through wedding magazines and dream of our perfect
man. I deeply wanted him and the life we were building
together.

His dad was a powerful, brilliant, thick-skinned man with
an illustrious career and tumultuous past. He was a straight
shooter at the best of times and he became more direct as
he came to terms with his condition.

I found myself in his bedroom, a spacious room on
the second floor of his tall brick home in an affluent
neighbourhood in Toronto. His room smelled of tobacco
and newspapers. The crisp white pillows were stacked
behind his head, books and plates of half-eaten food
strewn on the bed beside him. I sat in a tall wing-backed

chintz chair at his bedside, ready to dazzle him with my charming personality.

I held myself on the edge of the chair, leaning in, searching for his approval.

Partway through our conversation, he stopped me and said "Erin, just stop trying so hard." Baffled and thrown off, I said nothing and politely left the room.

Later I raged with Sean, wondering what I had done wrong. What Sean's dad said went against everything I had been raised to do. I was taught to engage, lead the conversation, ask open-ended questions, and always contribute as much as possible.

My manners, my great conversational skills, my bubbly personality were key parts of my contribution, how was this "trying too hard"?

I felt so misunderstood.

It was years later—and after many more failed attempts at charming people—that the lesson sunk in. In my effort to have him approve of me and like me, I lost all access to my authenticity. My trying hard masked the real me.

It seemed counterintuitive at the time, yet experience has taught me that I am not here to win people over. I'm here to witness people. When "trying hard" is replaced with presence, things get very real and begin to flow.

I feel such gratitude for this experience with him now. I realize that there was nothing to show, nothing to tell, nothing to gain approval over. The lesson taught me to be fully with myself first so that I can fully be with others.

In my experience, I was trying to get approval. My focus was on what I can get over what I can give.

Getting real means being present with your true self. This is NOT a role you play, a position you hold, or an identity you are polishing. The truth is, over-efforting is unproductive. Getting real creates flow.

Remembering who you truly are can be accessed by recalling who you were when you were a child. Feel the innocence, the joy, the naturalness that you so fully embodied when you were young. Breathe deeply into this part of you and let it come alive. This is who you really are now.

Be the presence,
not the person.

— ZEN THINKING

THE PRACTICE

How would people describe who you were when you were
a child?

When you feel yourself over-effort, where do you feel in
your body?

When do you feel the loss of peace and the authenticity
drain out of you?

What will help you remember to pause?

When you feel yourself over-effort, what are you trying
to get?

You become. It takes a long time.
That's why it doesn't happen often to
people who break easily, or have sharp edges,
or who have to be carefully kept. Generally,
by the time you are *real*, most of your hair
has been loved off, and your eyes drop
out and you get loose in your
joints and very shabby.

But these things don't matter at all,
because once you are *real*, you can't be ugly,
except to people who don't understand.

- MARGERY WILLIAMS BIANCO

The Velveteen Rabbit

FIVE

BE A FOUNTAIN
NOT A DRAIN

BE A FOUNTAIN NOT A DRAIN

My mum was always a fountain of inspirational stories, fun facts, interesting articles, and ideas on ways to live. She was always energized. Honestly, I struggled to keep up with her simply walking down the street.

She lived in a home that was narrow with several flights of stairs. I never knew her to walk up or down, she flew. It was as though she felt there was no time to dawdle. Life was a fountain of wonderment around her and she wasn't going to miss a thing.

I never knew her to complain or whine and she didn't put up with my complaining or whining either. She did this through a cheerful reminder that no matter what, in life we can choose to be either a fountain or a drain. It's up to us how we want to experience our life.

This choice wasn't always so clear to me.

When Sean and I got married, I was 34 years old and knew I wanted kids. We got pregnant right away, my plan was afoot. I immediately began preparing for this little being who would complete our family. My mind raced out into our future, pushing a stroller, sipping coffee, mummy and me music lessons, that intoxicating baby smell filling my soul. Our baby, newly conceived, was already loved.

The announcements were made, the plans laid, the future was bright. Until it wasn't. At almost 14 weeks, during an ultrasound, I discovered the baby had no heartbeat. The days that followed were a blur. It was as though my entire life went dark. All my hopes and dreams were attached to this little being that was suddenly no more.

At the time, I was working as a Designer and Brand Manager at a company I helped build. I shared an office with Stacey, an account manager who was kind, diligent, and pragmatic. Within a week of returning to work after my miscarriage, she announced to us all that she was pregnant. My heart sank. I had to share an office with her and watch her blossom and bloom while I wilted and withered.

My boss Danielle, dynamic, powerful, and my creative mentor, was tender and empathetic. She had all the time in the world for me and held big space as I navigated the pain of miscarriage. She was patient, until I became a drain.

The longer it took me to get pregnant again the more I became resentful toward Stacey. Watching her belly grow was a daily reminder that mine wasn't. I assumed that because I got pregnant so quickly the first time it would happen like that again. But month after month, test after test, I still wasn't pregnant.

As tension grew around the office, Danielle was the one to put an end to it. She rolled up her office chair to mine, spun me around to face her, put her hands on my knees and looked me in the eye. I will never forget the words she said next. "Erin, if you keep this up you will lose all your friends." I had become a drain.

Danielle created a "wake-up" moment for me. She had the courage to tell me the truth. I will forever be grateful to her for that.

I recognized that I had the opportunity to become a fountain in my life simply by seeing the impact I had on people and changing my view. Instead of looking down the drain, I looked up and began to see ways I could help myself. I started to create ways I could experience progress even in the face of disappointment.

A year later, I became pregnant again, nine months later I gave birth to Luke. The moment I held him I experienced love like I'd never experienced before. It was worth the wait because ever since that moment my life has been a technicolour fountain, full of joy and deep love.

The fountain is a source of creativity. The fountain produces wonderful things in life while the drain only sucks. When I pause and look at what I've created in my life I am reminded that the fountain is abundant, limitless and always available.

Being a fountain is not about rainbows and unicorns, it's about seeing the abundance available everywhere. The simple analogy that my mum provided gave me a framework to see how I was being for others, and for myself.

Being disappointed, feeling upset, experiencing lows are all part of the human experience. It's important to acknowledge and to fully experience the wide spectrum of feelings and not allow them to pull you down the drain.

ERIN ANDERSON

THE PRACTICE

In my life, where am I being a fountain?

In my life, where am I being a drain?

What do you need to do, see, say or create to shift from drain to fountain?

What proof of wonderment can I see right now?

What proof of joy can I see right now?

You'll see it
when you believe it.

- DR. WAYNE DYER

SIX

PERFECT IS BORING

PERFECT IS BORING

My mum lived by the phrase carpé diem. She was a force of nature, always creating, engaging, and connecting. I've never known anyone who was as unstoppable as she was. She was an artist, teacher, painter, writer, poet, world traveler, and philanthropist.

In the final days of her life, she realized that her bucket list was checked off and that she felt totally complete.

I'm moved every time I think about how peaceful she was before dying. She said everything she wanted to say, did everything she wanted to do. No regrets.

Did she have it easy? Was everything handed to her? No, not at all. In fact, her life circumstances were stacked against her. She simply understood that life was to be created by her and no one else. Yet she didn't do it alone. She valued her family, community, and teachers. She sought out help and the guidance to take her work and life to the next level.

I think of her when I feel doubtful. I start to question my "good enoughness" and a sense of fatigue sets in. Doubt leads me to hesitate to do something because I start thinking, "it's not perfect so why bother." If I zoom ahead to the end of my life, I want that feeling of being totally complete. I can't imagine saying, "I did only a few things on my bucket list, but I did them perfectly."

One of my favourite things to do with my mum was to wander through art galleries and listen to her generate incredible insights about art. If I ever said "I don't like that one" she would correct me to say "I don't respond to that one." The artist doesn't strive to be perfect and liked, the artist strives for a response.

Perfect lives in a box. Perfect is sign, sealed, and delivered with all the edges smoothed over. There is nothing to discover, nothing to learn, nothing to press up against in perfect. The experience is over in seconds.

The world needs to see your work of art, your life. Don't wait until it's perfect to put it out there because perfect is boring.

Love yourself through this process. Remind yourself how good, whole, and complete you are, no matter what. You are a work of art.

THE PRACTICE

The desire for things to be perfect is an excuse that harms you and blocks your ability to show up and contribute fully. You will know if you start going down the perfection tunnel when anxiety and doubt set in. You'll feel it in your body as constriction, an energetic block in the road.

When your need to be perfect sets in, you only notice the dirty windows instead of seeing the beautiful views.

To step out of this, ask yourself a new question to help shift your focus away from the fringe details that seem to be all-consuming.

SHIFT YOUR FOCUS

What's at the core of what I want?

What is most important in my big picture?

As the witness of my life, what is truly working right now?

What is one thing I can do now that would excite me?

A lifetime is like a flash of lightning in the summer sky. Knowing this, may I be well and happy, may I be peaceful and calm, may I be protected from dangers, and may my mind be free from hatred.

– GAUTAMA BUDDHA

SEVEN

CONTRIBUTION HAPPENS IN THE NOW

CONTRIBUTION HAPPENS IN THE NOW

My parents created a trekking company in Nepal. For 30 years, they brought small groups into the high altitude of the Himalayas. I was fortunate enough to go with my dad on several expeditions and led a few of my own. It was on the trails, at high altitude with elements out of our control that I learned true leadership. It was with the people who seemingly had so little that I learned what true happiness looked like. It was in the face of hopelessness that I learned that true contribution happened in the present.

When my parents and I reflected on our times in Nepal, we often wondered how we could contribute to the world as much as we'd received from it.

My parents created programs and initiatives to support the people they loved so dearly. They dedicated their creativity and passion to writing a book and donating the proceeds to the Hope Disability Organization. Their book *Hasten Slowly* raised funds to provide wheelchairs, build ramps, and provide for much needed surgeries. Imagine living as a disabled person in a remote Nepalese village where there was no electricity and plumbing? The Hope Disability Organization seeks out people who are unable to move or care for themselves and helped restore dignity and freedom.

In 2018, my dad and I traveled to Pokhara, Nepal to meet with the organization leaders. The passionate and charismatic double-amputee, Ganga and her team were making heroic measures to help the lost and forgotten. I was vibrating with excitement to hear the stories and see the impact she and her team were making.

During our two-day stay with them, we talked about challenges the disabled were facing. Many fathers of children born with disabilities leave, not wanting to face the sacrifice and financial strain involved. We heard stories of children being sent to climb tall trees to collect food for the cows and becoming paralyzed as a result of falling from the tree tops. Ganga herself lost her lower legs from a kitchen fire. Sadly, this was a common story in Nepal.

We met with a family whose 14-year-old girl had spina bifida and desperately wanted to go to school. As we sat in her living room, the representatives from the helping organizations said "Sad, isn't it? Too bad there's nothing we can do."

Triggered by the lack of hope and possibility while sitting in her living room, I began to feel rage boil up within me. Here my dad and I were ready and willing to help and we are told there is nothing that we could do.

I turned to my dad, a veteran in the realm of contribution, and gave him a pained and puzzled look. He leaned back in his chair, calm as a monk.

Later I raged on about the injustice, the frustration of the situation, and the annoyance I felt when our good intentions were met by a wall.

He sighed and reminded me "One person at a time."

Getting mad took me out of being present with the people I was with. Frustration was a distraction away from seeing the people in front of me.

Contribution is now, right at this moment, and if we are distracted, we will miss it.

Remember that there is only one important time and it is NOW. The present moment is the only time over which we have dominion. The most important person is always the person with whom you are, who is right before you, for who knows if you will have dealings with any other person in the future? The most important pursuit is making that person, the one standing at your side, happy, for that alone is the pursuit of life.

- LEO TOLSTOY

THE PRACTICE

What helps you remain present?

What cause do you love to contribute to?

What are some conditions you accidentally put on your contributions?

What stops you from contributing?

CREATE A STATEMENT

Create a statement to align to your unconditional contribution. When you feel yourself not being present or feeling attached to an outcome, give yourself a grounding statement.

Here are a few examples:

I am free to give fully here and now.

I am here to contribute, unattached to the outcome.

I am pure love.

EIGHT

YOU ARE ALWAYS INFLUENCING

YOU ARE ALWAYS INFLUENCING

My mum was an influencer. She didn't rely on social media, fashion, or position in society to make a lasting and positive impact on people. She was known by the owner of the local coffee shop, by the hotel operator in Kathmandu, Nepal, by the guy at the vegetable stand. She looked them in the eye, asked them questions about their lives, and discovered their hidden gifts. She always left them feeling uplifted. To her, this was just good manners.

She loved her morning walks along Kits Beach in Vancouver with her dog Ruby. I joined her on many of these walks which always turned into a biography tour of the people that she met that day. There was the dancer with the Bichon Frisé, the mysterious cold water swimmer with a pug, the delightful woman from Greece with the golden retriever. She would stop and address each person by name, introduce me (every time) and ask them a specific question about their lives that would have their eyes twinkle and their back straighten. We would end up at the coffee shop where she'd have an electric exchange with the owner, Dawn. She'd get all the updates on her family and how business was going.

My mum's friends, family, and admirers counted on her vivacious and loving style. She was quick, witty, full of knowledge, and wildly generous.

"Manners matter" was her mantra, and she became known in our family as the captain of manners bootcamp. My kids lightheartedly learned ways to engage with people, how to ask open-ended questions, and how to hold a knife and fork. They knew never to chew gum in public and to enunciate their words.

There were many times I wanted her to lay off my kids. I just wanted them to like her. But when she died and the stories about her came out of their sweet mouths, I realized they loved her.

I may never fully know her influence on them, but I do know what her influence was on me. Elevating people, teaching, leading, sharing wisdom was her way of being. It was an act of pure generosity. She didn't hold back and in asking my kids to pronounce the letter "t" in ToronTo (not toronno), she influenced their lives. She ignored their obvious eye rolls when she'd usher them around parties introducing them to adults, making them look them in the eye, use their full name, and shake their hands.

The very definition of influence is the capacity to have an effect on the character, development, or behavior of someone or something. She knew who she was, she embraced her sage and shared from that way of being passionately. "Manners matter" was one of the many platforms she stood on with grace, commitment, and total belief.

After she died, I found a blog post I had written about how my mum influenced me printed in her desk drawer. It had a tea cup stain on it and had been folded up several times. On the back she wrote, "I'm glad it sunk in Erie!" I wondered if she meant to give me this note. I feel good knowing that she saw the influence she had on me.

I realized that we are all influencing, all of the time. Every word, every act, every non-action, all have the ability to influence another.

My mother chose the way she wanted to influence my kids. She was specific and laser focused. I'm certain that 15 years from now, if you ask my son Luke what influence his grandmother Gail had on him, he'd have a clear answer.

The truth is, you can be influential without manners. We've seen examples of this abound in the world.

What made my mum so special is that she understood that her influence was in how she conducted herself everyday, with everyone.

She chose how she wanted to be for others and she went all in.

Consider that you too are always influencing. Do you know how do you want to leave every person you meet? Influencing people is not a mask you wear or a show you put on.

My mum wasn't interested in building a reputation. She built her legacy one person at a time.

THE PRACTICE

BEING PRESENT TO YOUR INFLUENCE TAKES AWARENESS AND PRACTICE

What do you want to be known for right now?

What do you want to be remembered for when you die?

What are good manners to you?

How do you want to be treated by others?

You give but little when you give
of your possessions. It is when you
give of yourself that you truly give.

- **KAHLIL GIBRAN**

NINE

FORGIVE TO LIVE BIG

FORGIVE TO LIVE BIG

Forgiveness is an act of love, and it sets you free to live your big life.

It is only when you can be unattached from the outcome of another person or situation that no harm can come. Forgiveness allows us to forgive ourselves, the situations, the circumstance, the people who we perceive are causing us pain. It takes something to acknowledge what happened, forgive, and move forward. Unforgiveness on the other hand keeps us stuck.

Forgiveness, as is love, is complete, whole and unconditional.

As I reflect on my mother's life, I realize there were two things she rarely spoke of: gratitude and forgiveness. Despite the fact that she grew up with a disabled mother, lost her brother to suicide, and overcame cancer three times, I never sensed bitterness from her. Nor did I see her force gratitude on herself. Gratitude wasn't something she needed to practice, it was a result of her ability to forgive and live her life fully in the now.

It seemed as though she allowed the challenges to be tough, to be brutal even, but they never took her love away.

Forgiveness didn't come as easily for me. It took me many heartbreaks to understand and appreciate the power unforgiveness had. Yet I realize that it was those very heartbreaks that allowed me to truly know what love is and what love isn't.

The grudges, the holding on, the arrogance that I was 100% certain about a situation never served me. I may have been right about someone, but I never felt truly happy or free. Holding onto unforgiveness prevented me from living big.

The most profound witnessing of love and ultimate forgiveness in my life was the moment my mum died. She was surrounded by those who loved her deeply. My father held her hand; I sat at her feet.

In her last few moments, I remember saying "You've got this mum," encouraging her to leap into the next world. I couldn't believe the words coming out of my mouth. I wondered why I wasn't raging against her death, why I wasn't clinging to her life? I believe this is love's work.

I loved my mum and I miss her terribly, yet our relationship wasn't smooth sailing. In fact, I spent most of my life being triggered by her. She'd joke that "If it's not one thing, it's your mother."

She was quick to share her opinions and felt she was right about them. I would often argue with her and become wildly defensive, feeling like I needed to protect a boundary. Her opinions and judgments began to precede her. I could see her cleaning a dish in my sink and I'd snap thinking she's judging the way I keep my home. It became apparent that she could make no remark without it stinging her sensitive daughter.

What is this wiring that starts to fray between two people who love each other so dearly? What is this glitch in the system that blocks the joy? When it's left unattended, unforgiveness sets in.

In lighter moments, we'd joke that she was able to push my buttons because she installed them. A chuckle turned to a pensive thought with how true this really is.

The constriction of unforgiveness is like holding onto a heavy metal ball with spikes on it. The other end of the ball is attached to the person or situation you are harbouring resentment toward.

One thing I never considered until recently is that I can set the ball down. I didn't need to understand or even accept all that was happening on the other end.

The ineffective assumption is that forgiveness comes with a big heavy conversation explaining your point of view. This leads to blame, resentment and misunderstanding.

To forgive another is a soulful act. It can be a simple moment of recognizing you're carrying something heavy and it's time to set it down. Take a deep breath, choose to set yourself free.

Forgiveness is for you. It restores your peace, love, and vitality.

THE PRACTICE

Where in your body, do you hold the energy of a grudge?

Who would you like to forgive?

What situation from the past do you want to leave in the past?

What do you forgive yourself for?

How would it feel to release any unforgiveness?

To forgive is to set a prisoner free and discover that the prisoner was you.

- LEWIS SMEDES

TEN

TINY JOYS
CREATE A BIG LIFE

TINY JOYS CREATE A BIG LIFE

The tiny little joys in my day feel like an unexpected windfall, sudden and magical.

My daughter is sitting on her usual chair at the breakfast table, munching a bagel. I lean over and give her a kiss on her neck. A stolen tiny moment. I nuzzle in and breathe her in. Pure magic. I cannot believe I created her and that I get to be her mum. She loves this spot at the table. She watches me whiz around cleaning and cooking. We talk of tiny little things that delight us both.

She asks me for a banana, "The way I like it, mummy" she says. I'm her mum, I know exactly what she means. So I slice off the end and expertly carve a slice down the side of the banana and cut it up into inch thick pieces. Just the way she likes it.

These are the tiny little moments that make my life so full of joy. Like the smell of cinnamon on apples and seeing our toothbrushes side by side. She always says "Mummy, we are connected." And we are. Like how we both get a cold at the same time or when we both want to listen to the same music. These are the tiny little things that make my life so fulfilling.

My mother taught me how to be a mother. She didn't spoil me or buy me "stuff," she noticed things with me. She would point out the robins singing spring into the air. She would say "Oh Erie, look! There's a bird at the feeder! The birds bring me such joy!" She would show me how colours dance together in works of art. She would point out little grammatical or spelling errors that would make my writing better. The tiny things were a big opportunity for wonderment.

By cherishing the tiny joys, she taught me that life is art, stitched together by moments that matter.

The truth is, life is not made up of checking boxes. It is not created through the eyes of others, it is your life after all. Life is made up of tiny little moments that make your heart skip, make your knees buckle, or tickle your senses. Life is created in micro-moments that are outside of the box your ego wants to keep you in. Tiny little joys are at the fringe, on the outskirts of your ego.

A tiny little joy is a miracle. We have to be present enough not to miss them.

THE PRACTICE

Your brain creates new neural pathways every day by noticing tiny joys. You have opportunities to create joy freeways in your brain if you choose to.

List all the tiny things that bring you joy.

What is bringing you joy right now?

Dwell on the beauty of life.
Watch the stars, and see yourself
running with them.

– MARCUS AURELIUS

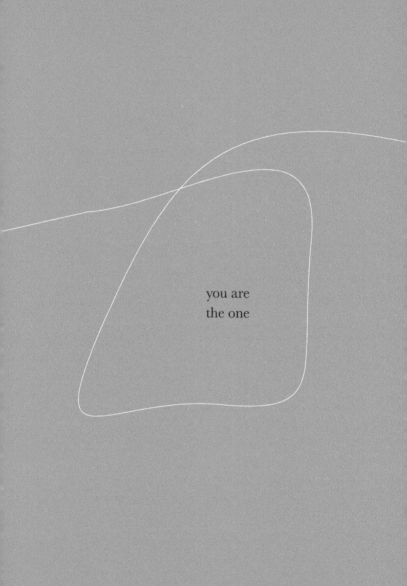

you are
the one